Meet the Author:

Hello my name is T'Pring Asencio, B.N.H., N.D. it is my pleasure to have the opportunity to author this book on Children's Health!

You will learn various conditions that children have, and how breast feeding can prevent these and many other conditions, and the long term effects on children whom are breastfed, and natural approaches to common childhood ailments.

Please note that this book is written on a Christian/ Naturopathic approach on some common childhood ailments. It is not intended to diagnose, treat, or cure any disease, or ailment. After each chapter there is a blank page for any notes you may want to write down.

The statements/recipes/herbs/therapies listed in this book have not been evaluated by the FDA.

Please visit my website at:

www.sunflowernaturopathyclinic.weebly.com

Or e mail me at drasencio11@gmail.com

"Children are little smiles put on Earth, for a Happy Blissful Future"

Dr. T'Pring Asencio

Table of Contents:

A Biblical verse about children

"Behold, children are a heritage from the LORD, the fruit of the womb a reward. Like arrows in the hand of a warrior are the children of one's youth. Blessed is the man who fills his quiver with them! He shall not be put to shame when he speaks with his enemies in the gate." (Psalms 127:3-5 ESV)

Chapter One
Common skin conditions

Eczema

What is Eczema?

The word "Eczema" can cause confusion. Many people use this word to refer to a common skin condition called atopic dermatitis. When this is the meaning, the words "eczema/atopic dermatitis" may be used.

However, the word "eczema" also has a more general meaning. Eczema can mean a family of skin conditions that causes the skin to become swollen,irritated, and itchy. Many skin conditions are considered a type of eczema.

Atopic dermatitis is one type. Other types include: Hand dermatitis, Contact dermatitis, Nummular dermatitis, and Seborrheic dermatitis. Dandruff is a mild type of Seborrheic dermatitis. Diaper rash and the rash that many people get after coming into contact with poison ivy are other types of 'eczema'.

Some of the symptoms include, but are not limited to:

☐ Flakey lesions

☐ Generalized redness

☐ Scaly and oozy

☐ Painful – Movement causes the skin to feel like is being stretched and torn.

What can be done to lessen the symptoms?

Aloe Vera

Shea Butter

Moisturizer

Fish Oil, (just to name a few)

All of these items can be found at a Health food store and promote moisturizing. Keep affected areas moisturized, and discourage child from scratching.

Eczema Ointment:
1 cup moisturizing lotion
1 tsp raw Shea butter
3 tsp Aloe Vera Powder
Mix everything together and store in a tight plastic container.

Acne

Acne is a common skin condition that can affect individuals of any age group, although it is more commonly noticed among teenagers and young adults. Acne develops when the follicle that carries dead skin to the skin surface becomes clogged. While acne in most cases is inflammatory, it can also develop as non-inflammatory acne.

It manifests itself as tiny pimples, papules, nodules, or cysts, as per the increasing nature of its severity. Typically, acne begins to show in the years following puberty, as this is when there are considerable hormonal changes that take place in the body.

Acne is also common among women due to monthly hormonal changes. Acne affects those areas of the skin that have the most number of sebaceous follicles. Thus, it is primarily visible on the face, chest, back, upper arms, and shoulders.

Typically, acne wanes off after the inflammation as the clogged pores subside, and acne outbreaks lessen once we get into our early twenties, as this is when the hormonal levels balance themselves out. In rare cases, however, medical investigation and follow up is required for treating acne of a more stubborn nature. Additionally, since each individual is physiologically different, it is possible that the acne may continue late into your thirties and forties.

While acne in itself does not pose any serious health risks, it could lead to scarring. Acne scars can, at times, be exceedingly stubborn, and may never really go away. Acne also has psychological implications as the acne and its scars are generally regarded as unappealing, leading to lowered self-esteem issues in teenagers and young adults.

Symptoms:

Acne symptoms include the presence of different types of pimples and cysts on the affected area of the skin. A pimple appears when the blocked pore begins to drain, so what is visible is usually the latter stage of acne. Some of the different physical indications of acne are as follows:

•Acne can manifest itself as enlarged hair follicles filled with sebum, which are referred to as comedones. Blackheads are comedones that pop out of the skin surface, and white heads are comedones that have not pushed their way through the surface of your skin.

•Papules are pink tender bumps on the skin and pustules are red at the bottom but filled with pus, owing to bacterial infection.

•Nodules are the large and painful, solid pimples that are deep seated in the skin, while cysts are the deep and painful pimples that are filled with pus and can develop scars in future.

Causes for Acne

Acne causes are many, and research is still being conducted in this arena. However, some of the common and established causes of acne are as follows:

•Many factors have been found to be contributive to acne development. In girls and women, the timeline during the menstrual cycle shows an increase in acne on the skin.

•Hormonal changes at the onset of puberty or during pregnancy can also cause the pores on the skin to get clogged up.

•A sudden start or stop in the use of birth control medication can also result in acne showing up on the skin.

•Heredity and the use of greasy cosmetics also results in the appearance of acne.

•Although a common myth exists that chocolates and oily food contribute to acne, this has not been scientifically proved yet.

•Teenagers and young adolescents show an increased manifestation of acne as the hormonal changes during puberty add to the sebum build-up, leading to more inflamed pores.

•Lifestyle changes, especially being subject to a lot of stress, can also result in acne developing on the skin.

Remedies for Acne:

Intensive research is been done in the field of dermatology to comprehend the nature, causes, and treatment for acne. Topical application of certain medications, use of certain home remedies, and changes incorporated into one's lifestyle help to decrease the intensity and subsequent outbreaks of acne.

Most people opt for various types of face washes and creams to deal with acne, and there are various products available in the market that promise acne-free skin. However, it should be kept in mind that these products do not completely eradicate the acne.

Face washes that contain salicylic acid help to drain the sebum from the clogged pores. Topical creams or gels can also be applied to dry or peel off a layer of skin or to restrict sebum formation.

Certain antibiotic creams can also be used to reduce the growth of acne causing bacteria. While some of these products can be bought over-the-counter, others may require the prescription of a qualified physician or dermatologist.

Apart from the conventional treatment, many people choose various home remedies to deal with acne. Natural and herbal remedies are becoming increasingly popular as these usually pose less risk of side effects, particularly for sensitive skin. Some of the commonly used herbal or home remedies for acne are as follows:

•Evidence suggests that aloe vera may be effective in treating minor skin infections, burns, cuts, as well as sebaceous cysts, pimples, and acne. These therapeutic effects can be attributed to the polysaccharides, anthraquinones, mannans, and lectins that are found in Aloe Vera. Applying Aloe Vera gel on the face and other acne-affected areas may thus be helpful.

•Honey is also another remedial option that can be used for acne treatment. Honey prevents the skin from becoming too oily, as an oily skin allows for more bacteria to thrive. At the same time, it helps maintain the moisture content of the skin. You can apply honey (mixed with yogurt) directly to your face or opt for honey-based face washes.

•A homemade face wash that contains diluted apple cider vinegar is also effective for clearing up acne. Apple cider vinegar is believed to help restrict bacterial activity on account of its antiseptic properties.

•Natural home remedies for acne include the use of face packs containing fenugreek paste or cucumber. Lemon juice diluted with mint and applied on the skin keeps infection at bay. Yogurt is also effective as it prevents the skin from getting too oily and supplies ample probiotics and nutrients to the skin.

For prevention and management of acne, a lifestyle change is also beneficial. Try to exercise regularly so that the pores on your skin remain open and clear. It also helps to get sufficient rest and to avoid sleeping on your face, especially if you are prone to acne. A healthy diet is also a requisite to keep acne at bay. Lastly, engaging in stress-relieving activities helps lower stress levels, decreasing the intensity of acne.

Various acne remedies at home can be used quite easily, and the results seen are often positive, with minimal side-effects. However, it is always best to consult a dietician or dermatologist before opting for any home treatment, as overuse or contraindications with other medications and treatments are possible. It is also best if you consult a physician if the redness and pain associated with acne takes a turn for the worse and does not subside.

Diet for Acne

The relationship between certain foods and the production of acne has not been scientifically established yet. However, a diet plan for acne would include lots of fresh fruits and vegetables and a sufficient intake of clean water. Almost all fruits and vegetables contain a good deal of vital minerals and vitamins. These help in keeping the skin clear as they provide the body with the necessary nutrients. In particular, vitamin A and B-complex vitamins are known to be beneficial for the skin.

Good sources of vitamin A include carrots, dark leafy vegetables, cantaloupe, red pepper, cayenne, dried apricots and herbs, as well as liver. For vitamin B, you can opt for dark leafy vegetables such as kale, spinach, chicory, collard greens, and Swiss chard, as well as legumes, egg yolks, whole-grain cereals, berries, and yeast. Keep in mind that too much of anything is also bad for health; a well-balanced diet plan is key. Also, if you're opting for vitamin supplements, then consulting a doctor is a must.

Suggestions for Acne

Adequate skin care is a requisite to keep acne development in check.

•Washing should be done gently and not more than twice or thrice a day, as frequent and strong washes irritate the skin further and this results in increased production of sebum. Pinching or pricking of the pimples also irritates the skin further and may result in scars that are difficult to get rid of.

•Although sunlight can help in drying the skin surface and making the acne look lighter, too much exposure of the skin to the harmful ultra violet rays of the sun does more harm than good.

•Shampooing your hair, especially if your hair type is oily, goes a long way in curbing the development of acne. This is because excessive oil in the skin is a breeding ground for bacteria that cause acne formation.

Notes

Chapter Two

The child who won't stay calm

What can be done by parents to help keep a child calm?

Have the parent try classical music.
I know if sounds funny, but I once took my child to a doctor's
appointment
and he was running everywhere and when the doctor put on classical
music
he was as calm as calm can be.

Try Chamomile
Chamomile can be made as a tea, or can be purchased as a supplement.

Keep the child busy
Have the child play outside. Have the child put things together. A child
that
is busy and focused will more likely be calm.

Withhold foods that are high in sugar.
Instead of giving the child products high in sugar, give them a naturally
sweetened snack. Sugar may make the child hyper in many cases. Sodas,
mixable drinks, etc are high in sugar. Try giving the child fruit juices, or
Coconut juice, water, etc. Cakes, cookies, etc., also have high sugar
content.
Alternative snacks include (but are not limited to): Raisins, Granola
bars, fruits, Sugar Free products.

Talk to the child
Ask him or her "why are you acting like this?"

They might simply be bored and are just acting out. Spend quality time with the child, and give them attention. Some children act out when they feel as if they are not getting
enough, or any attention.

Notes

Chapter Three

Childhood Obesity

Foods that are high in sugar, caffeine, fats will not only cause the child to become more hyper and aggressive, but it can lead to a more serious condition called *Child Obesity*. Weight management is a topic a lot of people very are sensitive to, so use tact, sympathy, and understanding when talking to your clients about it.

Today's society has over 40% more overweight people than it did 20 years ago. Children are eating more fatty foods, sweetened foods, junk foods, etc, than ever before. Obesity can lead to several other medical conditions as the child gets older.

Children do not go outside and play like they did 20 years ago, many children stay at home watching television, and eating junk foods, or playing video games which is not conducive to weight management, peak physical condition or good health.

Ways to keep a child in shape:
Have them play outside at least 1 hour per day
Give them fresh fruit or vegetables as a snack
Have them ride their bikes, play ball etc.
Cook healthy meals.
Avoid fried foods
Avoid caffeine
Stay away from high sugar content foods like: cakes, candies, cookies, ice cream, soda pop etc.

Notes

Chapter Four
Croup

Croup is a childhood illness usually caused by a group of viruses called Human Para influenza viruses, which also cause the common cold. The main symptom of croup is a "barking" cough, sometimes likened to the barking sound a seal makes. Croup can be serious enough to require treatment in a hospital. Up to 6% of children with croup are hospitalized, but it is very rarely fatal. For severe cases, treatment helps to keep the sick child breathing
normally until the infection ends. A case of croup typically lasts about one week.

It's estimated that six in 100 children get Croup each year. Children who get it tend to be younger than 6 years old, and it's seen most frequently in 2-year-old children.

What can be done? Below are 2 recipes for Croup tea:

CROUP TEA#1
2 teaspoons elecampane root
2 teaspoons Seneca snake root
2 teaspoons sage
2 cups water
Combine the above herbs in a pan and cover with the water; bring to a boil;
reduce heat, and simmer for 30 minutes; cool and strain. Take as needed.

CROUP TEA#2
1 teaspoon mullein leaves
2 teaspoons chopped valerian root
1teaspoon passionflower
2 teaspoons wild cherry bark
2 cups boiling water

Combine the herbs in a glass container and cover with the boiling water; steep for 30 minutes; cool and strain. Take as needed.

Notes

Chapter Five

Breast Feeding

A Biblical verse about breastfeeding:
Psalms 22:9...”You made me hope and trust when I was on my mother's
breast.”

Breastfeeding is one of the most natural and beneficial acts a mother can do for her child. Dramatic health benefits have been proven to pass from mother to child through breast milk; from antibodies which protect an infant at birth, to the exclusive nutrients in mothers' milk which have been shown to prevent a number of childhood diseases...the benefits are incalculable.

There is no other single action by which a mother can so impact the present and future health of her baby. Yet, in today's society, breastfeeding is often thought of as unnecessary.

Young mothers are mistakenly led to believe that formula does very well as a replacement for breast milk. It emphatically does not! Nothing can duplicate the properties of breast milk, no matter how many vitamins, minerals and supplements are added to what is basically a chemical formulation.

Breast milk remains the one and only natural, complete and complex nutrition for human infants.

It is nature's formula for ensuring the health and quality of life for infants, as well as on through childhood to adult life.

Just as importantly, breastfeeding promotes a very special bond between mother and child that only a mother can provide.

To fully understand the benefits of breastfeeding, these are some of the major, but by no means all, of the benefits of breastfeeding a baby:

Breastfeeding Facts: Health Benefits to Babies Who Breastfeed
☐ Children receive the most complete and optimal mix of nutrients & antibodies

☐ The varying composition of breast milk keeps pace with the infant's individual growth and changing nutritional needs

☐ Have fewer incidences of vomiting and diarrhea in the US (20-35 million episodes of diarrhea occur in children under the age of 5, resulting in over 200,000 hospitalizations and 400-500 deaths in the U.S.)

☐ Protection against gastroenteritis, necrotizing enterocolitis

☐ Reduced risk of chronic constipation, colic, and other stomach upsets

☐ Reduced risk of childhood diabetes

☐ Protection against ear infections, respiratory illnesses, pneumonia, bronchitis, kidney infections, septicemia (blood poisoning),

☐ Protection against allergies, asthma, eczema, and severity of allergic disease

☐ Reduced risk of SIDS (sudden infant death syndrome) Statistics reveal that for every 87 deaths from SIDS, only 3 are breastfed.

☐ Protection against meningitis, botulism, childhood lymphoma, Crohn's disease and ulcerative enterocolitis

☐ Decreased risk of tooth decay (cavities)

☐ Nursing promotes facial structure development, enhanced speech, straighter teeth and enhances vision.

☐ Breastfed infants develop higher IQ's, and have improved brain and nervous system development; IQ advantage of 10-12 points studied at ages
8, 12, and 18. (Breastfeeding is considered the 4th trimester in brain growth
and development...there are specific proteins in human milk that promote
brain development)

☐ Reduced risk of heart disease later in life

☐ Increased bone density

☐ Breastfeeding plays an important role in the emotional and spiritual development of babies

☐ Breastfed babies enjoy a special warm bonding and emotional relationship with their mothers

☐ Decreased risk for childhood obesity

☐ Are hospitalized 10 times less than formula fed infants in the first year of life

☐ The Colostrum (first milk) coats the GI tract, preventing harmful bacteria and allergy -triggering protein molecules from crossing into baby's blood

☐ Decreased risk for vitamin E and Iron deficiency anemia

☐ Decreased risk for acute appendicitis, rheumatoid arthritis, inguinal hernia, pyloric stenosis

☐ there are factors in human milk that destroy E coli, salmonella, shigella, Streptococcus, pneumococcus....and many others.

Here are some health benefits to Mothers Who Breastfeed

☐ Reduced risk of breast, ovarian, cervical, and endometrial cancers

☐ Reduced risk of anemia

☐ Protection against osteoporosis and hip fracture later in life

☐ Reduced risk of mortality for women with rheumatoid arthritis (RA) has been associated with total time of lactation

☐ Helps the mother's body return to its pre-pregnancy state faster – promotes weight loss...1/2 of calories needed to manufacture milk is pulled from fat stores... can burn from 500 - 1,500 calories per day.

☐ Helps delay return of fertility and to space subsequent pregnancies

☐ Develops a special emotional relationship and bonding with her child

☐ Breast milk is free- reducing or eliminating the cost of formula (in the thousands of dollars/per year), and is best for the baby

☐ Breastfed babies are sick less thus reducing healthcare costs to family in Doctor Office visits, prescriptions, over the counter medicine purchases, and hospitalizations

☐ Moms miss less time from work due to child related illnesses

☐ Helps the uterus contract after birth to control postpartum bleeding Other Benefits from Breastfeeding

☐ Breastfeeding makes you feel good. The hormones produced during nursing have an endorphin effect giving you a relaxed feeling.

☐ You have a great excuse to sit down and relax.....

☐ You can nurse while sleeping...nursing moms get more rest than formula feeding moms.

- Breastfeeding saves moms about 7 hours a week off their feet.
- No screaming baby in the middle of the night waiting on the formula to heat up.
- It's the only time you can ever lose weight without dieting or exercise!
- Breastfeeding is more convenient, when traveling, all you need is to take diapers, the milk is always available, sterile, and the right temperature.
- During times of disaster, you don't have to worry about finding formula.
- Breastfed babies smell great....spit ups don't stain, or smell, and poopie diapers are not offensive...(until solids are introduced)
- Breastfed babies know their moms and will never confuse them with a sitter.
- The strong bond developed with nursing is much more intense.
- There is no feeling to describe the child suckling at your breast and letting go to give you a big smile; and knowing that the growth of your baby came from what your body produced! Wow! What a feeling!
- The satisfaction of knowing you are giving your baby the best start in life!
- Breast milk taste great! Sweet tasting! Variations in taste according to foods mom eats. Formula tastes the same and is awful!
- Breastfeeding requires the use of only one arm....you can do other things while breastfeeding, (except cooking and driving)

Notes

Chapter Six

Hay Fever & Allergies:

An allergy is a hypersensitive reaction to a normally harmless substance.

There are a variety of substances, termed *'allergens'* that may trouble a sensitive individual.

This section addresses respiratory allergies, both chronic and seasonal. Home remedies for allergies can help reduce and treat allergies symptoms. Common allergens include pollen, animal dander, house dust, feathers, mites, chemicals, and a variety of foods. Some allergies primarily cause respiratory symptoms; others can cause such diverse symptoms as headache, fatigue, fever, diarrhea, stomach ache, and vomiting.

If a child has allergies, he/she may suffer from a stuffy and/or runny nose, sneezing, itchy skin and eyes, and/or red, watery eyes. Needless to say, it can be very uncomfortable. Generally one will not suffer any of these side effects by using home remedies for allergies.

Whether allergies are seasonal or chronic depends on the particular allergen or allergens involved. Seasonal allergies tend to be caused by pollen. Ongoing or chronic allergies are usually caused by factors that are present in the environment year-round, such as animal dander, dust, or feathers.

Common allergens include pollen, animal dander, house dust, feathers, mites, chemicals, and a variety of foods. Some allergies primarily cause respiratory symptoms; others can cause such diverse symptoms as headache, fatigue, fever, diarrhea, stomach ache, and vomiting. Home remedies for allergies can help reduce and treat allergies symptoms.

Chronic allergic rhinitis is a persistent inflammation of the mucous membrane lining the nasal passages that is caused by an allergic reaction. It is characterized by a stuffy, runny nose, frequent sneezing, and a tendency to breathe through the mouth. The eyes may be red and watery. Headache, itchiness, nosebleeds, and fatigue may be secondary complications. Dark
circles under the eyes (called "allergic shiners"), along with a puffy look to the face, are frequently seen.

Home remedies for Allergies - Diet

Home remedies for allergies #1: Drink lots of water to thin secretions and ease expectoration.

Home remedies for allergies #2: If the child has respiratory allergies, they may be allergic to certain foods. In addition to dairy products and wheat, common culprits include eggs, chocolate, nuts, seafood, and citrus fruits and
juices. Try eliminating one of these foods for two weeks and watch for an improvement. Use an elimination or rotation diet to discover and work with food allergies.

Home remedies for allergies #3: Try eliminating dairy foods from the diet. Dairy foods can thicken mucus and stimulate an increase in mucus production. If allergies are seasonal, it may also be helpful to avoid whole wheat during the allergy season; many allergy sufferers are sensitive to wheat.

Home remedies for allergies #4: Eliminate out cooked fats and oils. When the body is under any type of stress, including the stress of an allergic reaction, the digestive system is not as strong as usual, and fats, which are difficult to digest at the best of times, can put a strain on the digestive system. Also, undigested fats contribute to mucus production and foster a toxic internal environment.

Home remedies for Allergies - Supplements

Home remedies for allergies #5: Calcium and magnesium are important nutrients for the allergy sufferer. They help to relax an over reactive nervous system. While symptoms are acute, take a supplement containing 750 to 1,000 milligrams of calcium and 500 milligrams of magnesium twice a day.
Then take the same dosage once a day for two months.

Home remedies for allergies #6: Allergies are often related to the transformation and transportation of foods in the digestive system. Taking a digestive-enzyme supplement will enhance the assimilation and utilization of nutrients. Take a full-spectrum digestive-enzyme supplement providing 5,000 international units of lipase, 2,500 international units of amylase, and 300 international units of protease, plus 500 to 1,000 milligrams of
pancreatin immediately after each meal.

Before we continue, this might good place to discuss calculating child
dosages for supplements or herbs (except teas):

Weight of child
_____
= Fraction of adult dose
150 lbs

(Average adult weight)
Example: Child weighs 50 lbs., what percentage of the recommended dose would you
give?

50 lbs 1
_____ = ____
150 lbs 3 of the adult dose

~~~~~~

Home remedies for allergies #7: Methylsulfonylmethane (MSM) is a good source of sulfur, a trace mineral that may help to reduce the severity of the allergic response. Take 500 milligrams three or four times daily, with meals.

Home remedies for allergies #9: Vitamin C has anti-inflammatory properties. During acute flare-ups, take 1,000 milligrams five times a day for four to five days. Follow this with 1,000 milligrams three times a day for three weeks; then take 1,000 milligrams a day for two months. Some people
with allergies find mineral ascorbate vitamin C or esterified vitamin C (Ester-C) easier to tolerate than simple ascorbic acid.

Home remedies for Allergies - Herbs

Home remedies for allergies #10: If your nasal mucus is green or yellow, you may have an infection on top of allergies. Take one dose of an Echinacea and goldenseal combination formula supplying 250 to 500 milligrams of Echinacea and 150 to 300 milligrams of goldenseal two to three times daily for five to seven days to help resolve the infection.

Home remedies for allergies #11: Nettle can be very helpful for drying out the sinuses. It can be highly effective for chronic allergies. Take 150 to 500 milligrams two or three times daily, as needed, for two weeks.

Home remedies for allergies #12: Turmeric is an East Indian herb with natural anti- inflammatory properties. It is an excellent remedy for those who suffer from fatigue coupled with allergies. Take 250 milligrams three times daily.

Notes

Chapter 7
Focus and paying attention

This seems to be a common problem in today's society amongst children, and it can seem to get frustrating. Believe it or not there are ways that you can help the child focus and pay attention. Here are some suggestions you can give parents or care givers:

How to help a child focus

Give simple instructions, one step at a time. Telling a child with attention problems to clean his room may backfire, causing him to become overwhelmed and even less able to focus on the task. Instead, tell him to put all the dirty clothes in the hamper. When that's done, give him the next job, like picking up all the toy cars, and so on, until the overall task is completed.

Make a journal with a page for each task she does on a regular basis. Include one page for homework, one for chores, and another for other responsibilities. Write down each step in sequence and have your child refer to it as she works.

Identify triggers that are distracting and remove them. Some kids need to work on their own away from the chatter of classmates. Others need to face away from windows or doors. Clear the child's desk of everything but the tools he needs to complete his work. Allow the child to have move around and offer him "fidget tools."

An item like silly putty or a squishy ball can actually allow him to focus on the task at hand.

Standing or walking around while he's listening or working may help him concentrate.

Get down to the child's level and look her in the eye when you talk to her. Keep instructions brief and simple, and ask her to repeat what you've said to be sure she heard and understood.

Provide opportunities for the child to burn off energy. Activities like dance and martial arts help kids learn to focus and use up excess energy, but simply running around in the yard before beginning a task that requires focus can also help.

Below is a list of positive abstracts for a child who needs help focusing…

Cranberry
Broccoli
Peppermint
Onion
Plantain
Almond
Apples
Celery
Strawberry
Honey
Persimmon
Rose hips
Grape juice
Cabbage
Pistachio
Prune
Cauliflower
Aloe
Peas
Brussels sprouts
Acai
Kiwi
Lemon/lime
Mango
Cherry
Ginkgo
Go tu kola
Cinnamon
Walnut
Peach
Cod liver oil

Okra
Exercise
Grapefruit
Eggplant
Saint John's Wort

Notes

Chapter 8

Fever/ Seizures

What is a Fever?

- A fever is a body temperature higher than a normal temperature of 98.6° F.
- Fever is a healthy way in which the body fights infection.
- What could happen if a Fever will not go down in temperature? Possible Seizure

Some Facts

Fevers seem to be the most worrisome in children less than 3 months of age. At this age, a child with a rectal temperature of 100.4° F or greater should be seen by a physician.

When a child has a fever, the main concern is how sick your child seems. This is much more important than the height of the fever. High fevers are not usually dangerous. The height of the fever alone does not indicate the seriousness of the infection.

- Temperature strips on the forehead are inaccurate.
- Ear thermometers aren't very reliable in children less than 6 months of age, or for temperatures over 102° F.
- High fevers do not cause brain damage unless greater than 107° F or associated with diseases that affect the brain, like meningitis (an infection of the fluid that covers the brain and spinal cord).
- Do not give any medicines to infants younger than 2 months of age with a fever without notifying your doctor's office first. If the infant is less than 3 months of age, if the infant feels warm, take a **rectal** temperature, which is definitely the most accurate method for infants. Call your doctor immediately if the temperature is 100.4° F or greater. If the infant is bundled, this can cause an

elevated temperature. Unwrap the infant and retake the temperature in a half hour.

- Breathing rates and heart rates are increased with a fever.
- Seizures associated with fevers only occur in about 3 to 5 percent of the population and these are called febrile seizures. They are generally harmless.
- Teething does not cause a significant fever (not greater than 100.4° F).
- A common viral infection called roseola affects infants from 6 months to about 3 years of age. There is a fever for two to three days and then as the fever goes away, a rash develops. The rash is flat and pink or slightly raised dots. It looks like an intense heat rash. It is mostly on the neck and body and lasts one to two days. Once the fever is gone for 24 hours, the child is not contagious. There is no specific treatment for the rash. **About 10 percent of viruses cause fever and rash**.
- Fevers are usually caused by viruses or bacteria. Viruses are the most common cause of fever in childhood.
- External sources of heat can be dangerous. Heat illness occurs because of excess heat exposure. There is a range of severity of this disease. Mild symptoms can include muscle cramps, stomachache and headache. Heat stroke is a life-threatening emergency associated with temperatures over 106° F (41° C) and confusion, and is usually brought on by vigorous exercise in the heat.

What can be done naturally?

1) Fever reducing herbs

Several herbs have diaphoretic, or sweat-inducing, properties. By initiating or increasing perspiration, these herbs rid the body of the toxins contributing to the illness and help keep the fever from going too high. Thus, the healing is accomplished and the fever breaks.

Such common herbs as angelica, elderberry, rosemary, and yarrow are all diaphoretic. Drinking infusions of these will help the fever process. However, continued sweating can cause dangerous dehydration if you don't consume adequate fluids. Of course, it's important to support immune function during a fever. Use immune boosters such as echinacea, licorice, chamomile, goldenseal, or Oregon grape and foods rich in vitamin C and flavonoids.

When to seek a Pediatrician:

If a fever lasts more than three days or is above 102 degrees Fahrenheit for any fever in infants and children.

2) Less clothing

Children should not be over-bundled when they have a fever, as this tends to raise their temperature. Dress infants in a minimum of clothes and use a light blanket if they have chills. Sometimes, an overbundled infant may have a slight elevation of temperature. If you suspect this, undress and retake their temperature in about one hour.

3) Sponging

Sponge baths are usually not necessary for low-grade fevers. Sponging may cause shivering and may be uncomfortable. Sponge baths may be useful with heatstroke, confusion associated with high fevers, or in children who are prone to febrile seizures. Never use alcohol or ice in the bath. Stop or raise the water temperature if the child is shivering. Lukewarm washcloths or sponges rubbed briskly over the skin with the child in two inches of water is the best technique.

4) Degree of sickness

How sick your child seems is more important than how high the fever is running. To assess how sick a child is when he or she has a fever, give an appropriate dose of acetaminophen or ibuprofen (see chart below), and see how he or she is behaving about one to two hours after the dose. The fever may not necessarily return to normal but is often lower. Keep in mind that some children can be seriously ill without any fever. The behaviors listed below probably indicate that a baby or child is **not seriously ill**.

- A baby will coo, make eye contact, smile or reach for an object.
- A toddler will pay attention to activities, smile, walk around to get things.
- An older child will engage in quiet activities like coloring or reading.

The behaviors listed below **may indicate a serious illness** despite fever reduction.

- A baby is not making eye contact, continuously cries and cannot be comforted.
- A toddler refuses to play, cries inconsolably, moans, appears very weak, turns away and stares repeatedly, or is very hard to awaken if sleeping.
- An older child refuses to talk and won't interact or is unable to get out of bed.
- The child keeps falling asleep without periods of activity; remember, sick children do tend to sleep more.

5) Promote liquids and rest

We all need to sleep more whenever our bodies fight an infection. Liquids are important because we sweat more when we have fevers. Children are more prone to dehydration compared to adults.

Signs of dehydration in children include:

- No urine output in 8 to 12 hours
- Listlessness
- Dry cracked lips and/or mouth
- No tears when crying

Immediately seek medical advice if:

- The child is younger than 3 months old and has a temperature of 100.4° F or greater.
- The child is constantly crying, irritable, inconsolable and behaving sick. (If possible, decide if your child is sick an hour after giving him or her acetaminophen or ibuprofen.)
- The child is drooling more than usual and having difficulty swallowing.
- The child has a stiff neck or headache and fever.
- The child has purple spots on the skin that are large or pinpoint, and do not fade with pressure.
- The child has difficulty breathing, unless it is due to a stuffy nose.
- The child is difficult to arouse, confused or delirious.
- The child is having his or her first febrile seizure.

Seek proper medical care at once if:

- Fever lasts more than four days
- Other symptoms include an earache, sore throat, urinary burning or frequency or persistent cough
- Fever is more than 100.4° F, especially if the child is younger than 2 years old.
- If the proper medical care is not made the fever may increase in temperature and cause a Seizure.

There are several types of Seizures some can be harmful, and some not.

One type of Seizure that is typically harmless is called:

Febrile Seizures:

These are usually harmless and occur most often from 5 months to 5 years of age, although they may occur after 6 years of age. There is often a family member who had febrile seizures as a child. They occur in about 3 percent to 5 percent of the population. Typically, the seizure occurs when the fever is rapidly increasing. They are typically brief, lasting only three to five minutes.

They may happen with any type of infection that causes a fever. These brief febrile seizures do not cause brain damage.

Any first febrile seizure should be evaluated by a physician to rule out the possibility of meningitis or other serious illness.

Because a child has a history of febrile seizures does not mean he or she will have epilepsy as an adult.

The treatment involves controlling the fever aggressively with herbal remedies. Some children with complicated, frequent or prolonged febrile seizures require prescription anti-seizure medicines.

Generalized seizures

This includes the convulsive, tonic-clonic, or Grand mal, type of seizures which people are most familiar, in which a child falls down and has jerking movements. Other types of generalized seizures include **atonic seizures**, which cause 'drop attacks', and **absence seizures** (petit mal). Absence seizures cause a brief loss of awareness and are one of the causes of staring spells. These staring spells are usually brief, lasting only about 10-15 seconds, with a return to normal awareness after the seizure and they may occur several times a day. Absence seizures can be brought on by hyperventilation and they have a characteristic EEG, with a 3-per-second spike and wave pattern.

Partial seizures

These generally have a focal or local onset (starting in the right leg, for example, in contrast to a generalized seizure, which begins in all parts of the body at the same time). Partial seizures may be **simple**, in which there is no loss of consciousness, including seizures in which a child jerks one arm or deviates his eye to one side.

Children can also have **partial complex seizures**, which also have a focal onset, but which do involve a loss of consciousness. They are similar to absence seizures in that they also cause staring spells, but with partial complex seizures, the staring spell is usually longer, lasting about 30 seconds to several minutes and the child may be confused after the seizure. In addition to just staring, these children may seem confused during the episode and may wander around.

Below is a partial list of some herbs that may help with Seizures:

Chinese Ginseng

Mistletoe

Sage

Skullcap

Motherwort

Please study the chart below:

Temperature equivalents

CELSIUS	FAHRENHEIT
36.6	97.8
37.0 NORMAL	98.6
37.6	99.6
38.0	100.4
38.6	101.4
39.0	102.2
39.6	103.2
40.0	104.0
40.6	105.1
41.0	105.8

Notes

Chapter Nine

Juice Therapy

This therapy is designed for the child whom prefers juice rather than teas, capsules, oils, liniments, etc. Juicy Therapy is a very cost effective, less time consuming method to help with many common ailments.

The following recipes are based from the "Raw Food Diet", and should be prepared whole, fresh, uncooked, for best and maximum results.

On the next few pages you will find common ailments with juices that may help.

Juices for Common Ailments

Colds

Carrot, Beet, Cucumber

Carrot, Celery, Radish

Carrot and Spinach

Constipation

Carrot and Spinach

Carrot

Spinach

Fever

Grapefruit

Lemon

Orange

Sinus Trouble

Carrot and Spinach

Carrot, Beet, and Cucumber

Carrot

Headaches

Carrot and Spinach

Carrot, celery, parsley, and spinach

Carrot, lettuce, and spinach

Notes

Chapter Ten
Raw Food Diet

When it comes to a suitable diet for children and their health, and diet many questions are asked, and left unanswered.

What is the "Raw Food Diet?"

The answer is in the question. All foods are natural raw, uncooked foods. This is the diet Almighty God created our bodies for.

What can some benefits of having children on this diet?

Since everything is all natural with no added substances, chemicals, flavors, sugars, and the list goes on it can do the following;

Help with behavior issues

Eliminate food allergies

Eliminate the amount of Obese Children

Help the child maintain a healthy diet

The simplest raw foods can be the most appealing to children.

For example:

Fruits

Apples

Cantaloupe

Grapes

Watermelon

Bananas

Pears

Vegetables

Sugar snap peas

Green Beans

Squash

Baby Carrots

Cucumbers

Above is a partial list of common favorite raw foods popular with children. These foods can be cup up, and the child can use their hands to eat.

The ratio for the Raw Food Diet consumption is

85% Vegetables

15% Fruits

This may be challenging at first, but after some time the Child will get use to it.

Apart from serving the child finger food, there are two other great alternatives listed below:

Juices and Smoothies

There is an abundance of vitamins and minerals contained in raw juices and smoothies. Making these drinks with a combination of fruits and vegetables is one of the most effective ways to incorporate a variety raw food into a child's diet.

Balancing the fruits and vegetables also eliminates the need for adding sweeteners. Just by blending greens with fruits will give the child a healthy smoothie or juice. This is a great supplement/ alternative that can replace any meal throughout the day.

Strawberry Banana Smoothie

1 half Banana

2 Strawberries

½ cup green leafy vegetable of choice

Blend together. Serve

Natural Lemonade

1 Apple

1 Lemon

½ cup green vegetable of your choice

Blend together. Serve

Raw Foods for snacks

Raisins

Almonds

Cranberries

Blueberries

Granola

If mixed together this makes a wonderful Trail Mix.

What should you educate Client on?

Before advising the client to change their child's diet educate the parent on the diet, and benefits. You may also want to inform the parent to consult with their Physician about this change in diet.

As with any major dietary change, it is important to inform the Client/ parent to consult their physician and to monitor intake carefully to ensure proper nutrient intake.

Inform the client that there is a chance that being on a Raw Food Diet may develop a Vitamin B-12 deficiency after adhering to the diet for several years.

Simple solutions to this issue include daily B-12 supplements.

Notes

In conclusion,
There are so many different aspects of Children's Health, so many different ailments, remedies, etc. I hope that you have found my book to be informative on many common conditions that effect children.

Dr. Asencio
Traditional Naturopath

www.ingramcontent.com/pod-product-compliance
Lightning Source LLC
Chambersburg PA
CBHW050338290526
45785CB00006B/2544